D1709360

SPRAYING EQUIPMENT

Heather Moore Niver

WORDS TO KNOW

crop A plant that is grown for food.

dispense To sprinkle around.

drone A flying robot.

fertilizer Something added to soil to make plants grow better.

hydraulic Moved by water.

orchard An area to grow trees like fruit trees.

pressure Force or power that is put on another thing.

weed A plant that grows where it is not wanted.

CONTENTS

Farmers use sprayers to help protect and grow their crops.

Spray It!

Spraying equipment comes in handy on a farm. Sprayers help spread liquid. They can be used to squirt things like water, fertilizer, bug control, and weed killer on fields and crops.

FAST FACT
Sometimes bugs are controlled with dust! The machines are called dusters.

This bean leaf has been eaten by an insect.

Bug Off!

Farmers want to protect plants.
Nibbling insects, or bugs, can damage
crops. Sprayers dispense a mix of water
and other materials. They spray
fertilizer to help plants grow, too.

Early farmers used simple hand sprayers like this one.

Pests of the Past

Farmers have sprayed crops for a long time. Long ago, they made small hand sprayers called syringes. They sprayed to get rid of weeds. They also sprayed to keep plants healthy.

FAST FACT
Early farmers had to pick each insect off their plants!

Hagie sprayers are used by many farmers. They have improved a lot over the years.

Rolling Right Along

In 1947, a farmer named Ray Hagie saw a problem. It was hard to put pesticides and weed killers on fields. He invented the self-propelled sprayer. It did not need to be pushed or pulled.

FAST FACT
A pesticide is something farmers use to kill bugs and other things that hurt crops.

Some hydraulic sprayers are small enough for farmers to carry.

The Lowdown on Low-Pressure Sprayers

There are different kinds of sprayers. Hydraulic sprayers move liquid with pressure. Low-pressure hydraulic sprayers only spray a little at a time. The spray is not very powerful.

FAST FACT
Low-pressure hydraulic sprayers can help get rid of weeds and certain insects.

Large sprayers can cover many crops at once.

Under High Pressure

Other hydraulic sprayers use high pressure. These sprayers can spray a lot of liquid. High-pressure sprayers can reach tricky areas like orchards. In an orchard, all of the tree leaves are close together.

An air-blast sprayer is used to spray an orchard.

What a Blast!

Another kind of sprayer is an air-blast sprayer. It uses air. An air-blast sprayer uses a pump to move the spray. A fan shoots the spray into the air.

FAST FACT
Air-blast sprayers do not waste water like hydraulic sprayers do.

This tunnel sprayer is being used to spray
fruit trees.

Terrific Tunnel Sprayer

Spray sometimes floats away. It does not land on the plants and trees. A tunnel sprayer has three sides. The tunnel helps aim the spray on the plants.

Some farmers have started using drones to spray pesticides.

Big and Small

Some sprayers are small. They can be held in your hands. Other sprayers are huge. These sprayers work with tractors. The tractor pulls the sprayer behind it.

FAST FACT
Scientists are working on "smart" sprayers. They can tell when some leaves aren't sprayed.

Activity

Make a Super Sprayer

Let's get started! You might want to do this project outside.

You will need:
- Water
- Spray bottle
- Food coloring
- White or light-colored paper

Step 1: Fill your spray bottle with water.

Step 2: Add a couple drops of food coloring.

Step 3: Put the nozzle on.

Step 4: Shake to mix the water and color.

Step 5: Place your paper outside or on

newspaper. Draw a plant or tree on the paper if you want.

Step 6: Spray your paper in different spots.

You've tested your sprayer! Hang it up so everyone can check it out.

How does a sprayer work? Try it for yourself!

LEARN MORE

Books

Berne, Emma Carlson. *Sprayers Go to Work*. Minneapolis, MN: Lerner, 2019.

Borth, Teddy. *Machines on the Farm*. Minneapolis, MN: Abdo Kids, 2016.

Maimone, S. M. *Crop Sprayers*. New York, NY: Gareth Stevens, 2017.

Websites

Kids Tractors Working on the Farm
www.youtube.com / watch?v=9H6AB4g2Fc8
See how sprayers work in this fun computer model.

Tractors and Trucks for Children by Blippi
www.youtube.com / watch?v=4i7j2npFOtE
Learn about all kinds of farm tractors and trucks with this real-life video.

INDEX

Published in 2020 by Enslow Publishing, LLC.
101 W. 23rd Street, Suite 240, New York, NY 10011
Copyright © 2020 by Enslow Publishing, LLC.
All rights reserved.
No part of this book may be reproduced by any means without the written permission of the publisher.

Library of Congress Cataloging-in-Publication Data

Names: Niver, Heather Moore, author.
Title: Spraying equipment / Heather Moore Niver.
Description: New York : Enslow Publishing, 2020. | Series: Let's learn about farm machines | Includes bibliographical references and index. | Audience: Grades K-3.
Identifiers: LCCN 2019014641| ISBN 9781978513198 (library bound) | ISBN 9781978513174 (pbk.) | ISBN 9781978513181 (6 pack)
Subjects: LCSH: Spraying and dusting in agriculture--Juvenile literature. | Spraying equipment--Juvenile literature.
Classification: LCC SB953 .N58 2020 | DDC 632/.94--dc23
LC record available at https://lccn.loc.gov/2019014641

Printed in the United States of America

To Our Readers: We have done our best to make sure all website addresses in this book were active and appropriate when we went to press. However, the author and the publisher have no control over and assume no liability for the material available on those websites or on any websites they may link to. Any comments or suggestions can be sent by email to customerservice@enslow.com.

Photos Credits: Cover, p. 1 Eric Buermeyer/Shutterstock.com; interior pages background landscape Jurgis Mankauskas/Shutterstock.com; pp. 4, 14 © iStockphoto.com/fotokostic; pp. 5, 7, 9, 11, 13, 15, 17, 19, 22 (hay bale) photomaster/Shutterstock.com; p. 6 © iStockphoto.com/jess311; p. 8 Science & Society Picture Library/SSPL/Getty Images; p. 10 Bloomberg/Getty Images; p. 12 © iStockphoto.com/bluegame; p. 16 agrofruti/Shutterstock.com; p. 18 Malcolm Case-Green/Alamy Stock Photo; p. 20 Photomontage/Shutterstock.com; p. 23 Africa Studio/Shutterstock.com; cover, p. 1 logo element (tractor) Krivosheev Vitaly/Shutterstock.com.